The Beauty of Worship

In the Presence of the King

Dwendolyn Andrea Tatum

Publisher: Co-Author Network, LLC

Publishing Services: One Smart Lady Productions, LLC

Publishing Imprint: Gladstone Publishing Services

Revised cover design by Tia Cooke: https://www.cookeclassic.com

COPYRIGHT

CONTENTS

ACKNOWLEDGMENTS

I am so blessed and grateful that I finally gave birth to this book baby. It has been in the labor room since 2020. I received a prophetic word in 2018 that I would author a book. This book is a testimony to the faithfulness of God fulfilling His word.

There is so much truth in the statement, "I need you; you need me, we are all a part of God's body." (Lyrical Quote: I Need You To Survive – Hezekiah Walker)

I love and appreciate all the wonderful people I have had the honor to walk with on my incredible journey called "Life."

To my Heavenly Father God, who invited me into His majestic throne room to worship and fellowship with Him. It is an amazing place to be.

To my children Kyle and Kortnee Walker, my grandsons Andre' Love and Kyle Jr. (KJ)- a new addition to the family - and to his mom Shanique Wylie. I love you all from the bottom of my heart for your unconditional love and support.

To my Spiritual Mom, Rev. Dr. Jacqueline Reeves fondly known as "Rev. Jackie" and The Spoken Word Ministry, thank you for your unwavering support and continuous prayers that have covered me. Continue to rest in eternal peace.

To Evangelist Freda Sumlin-Williams, a dedicated, dear friend - thank you for your continued prayers, love, and support as you have walked alongside me. To your ministry, "Women at God's Table," thank you for your prayers.

To my writing coach, Michelle G. Cameron, thank you for your writing course, "The Writing Initiative," which ignited a fire within me to write and release what God had placed in my spirit. Also, I want to thank you for agreeing to edit my book.

To my other dear friends, Stephanie Miles, Pamella Leslie, Pastor Murvy Walcott, Robin Bright, Ellen Frye, William Collins, Minister Patricia Smargiassi, and Apostle Nabiyah Baht Yehuda. I am grateful for your love, friendship, and words of encouragement. Ingrid Anderson, thank you for your wise counsel that navigated me through some tough times. Marie Singletary, you always come through on time with the right words and resources. Your Ministry of Helps is truly a blessing.

A special thanks to Al and Linda Livingston, H. Corinne Beatty, Ms. Janie Carter, Anita and

Dwayne Dunham, Bridget and Rick Belton and all the Belton Family, I love you all.

In addition, a special thanks to:

Deidre E. Johnson, CEO of Blackberry Realty Group, who went above and beyond in assisting me to get settled and established back to my hometown in Charlotte, NC.

A special thank you to the members of St. Paul Presbyterian Church for warmly welcoming me into your family.

I would also like to acknowledge Emilio and Daniela Roman at Co-Author Network, LLC, for the inspiration, camaraderie and wealth of information, and the awesome platform that assisted me to complete my book. I appreciate you.

Lastly, I would like to thank the gifted and talented Publisher Deborah Smart, who is "one smart lady" for breathing her creative genius into the life of my book.

FOREWORD

I met Andrea Tatum a few years ago at a church that we both attended. I watched in awe as she waved banners during the services while dressed in colorful dancewear. I listened intently as she shared poetry that spoke about worship, and I worshipped as she sang her original melodies in praise to our God. Also, I had the privilege of watching her blow the shofar during worship.

I always thought that there was something very different about Andrea; she was quiet, but her heart for worship unto God was unmistakable. Worship is her heartbeat, and she is ready to share her heart with the world. Let us sit and learn about worship from a passionate banner bearer's perspective. I believe that her heart has shone through, and you will search the Scriptures to learn more about prophetic worship and spiritual warfare as you read, "The Beauty of Worship: In The Presence Of The King."

Michelle G Cameron

Author | Editor | Writing Coach

INTRODUCTION

"Worship God in the splendor (beauty) of His Holiness; tremble before Him all the earth." (Psalm 96:9, NIV)

Worship is not a new concept to the body of believers. All creation was formed and fashioned to worship the One who is greater, and who is above all things in the heavens and in the earth. God is, without a doubt, worthy of our praise and adoration. Our Heavenly Father has always desired to have an intimate relationship with His children. We catch a glimpse of His heart's desire to draw closer and commune with his children. In Exodus 8:1 (MSG), "God said to Moses, Go to Pharaoh and tell him God's Message: Release my people so they can worship me." He longed to

invite them close to Him into that place of one-
ness and intimacy, where they could experience
His loving presence.

So why do we worship God and often feel that
tug within our spirit to express our love and
adoration openly to Him? We were created to
worship God. Worship comes naturally when
we understand that the foundation of all worship is the great love of our Father; love respond-
ing to love. True worship shifts our attention
from ourselves and the cares of this world to our
loving Father. Our worship creates an atmosphere of gratitude and thanksgiving where God
can inhabit our place of praise.

As we acknowledge His lovingkindness through
our praise and worship, heaven invades earth and
ushers us into His gracious presence. God's presence and overwhelming love envelops us, which

in turn allows Him to unlock His blessings of miracles, healing, salvation, and deliverance.

> Praise the Lord, my soul, and forget not His benefits - who forgives all your sins and heals all your diseases, who redeems your life from the pit and crowns you with love and compassion.
>
> (Psalm 103: 2-4, NIV)

Our Heavenly Father is so gracious and loving that mere mortal words cannot describe His goodness and mercy.

When you come before the Lord with a surrendered heart of worship, you do not have to wait until Sunday morning, and you do not need a preacher. God is the Audience of One and He welcomes your praise in a place of love and intimacy as you celebrate His majesty and glory.

As you begin to feel and experience the manifest presence of the King of Glory, the program and the agenda is changed, and the norm is disrupted. It is with the utmost respect and reverence that we bow to the One who sits upon the throne of glory, dominion, and power.

"Who is the King of glory? The Lord strong and mighty, The Lord mighty in battle." (Psalm 24:8, NASB)

ENTER IN

I can recall, while in prayer, seeing a vision of a Golden Scepter being extended for me to touch. Then I heard a voice gently say to me, "You have permission to come into the presence of the King." These selections of songs are Holy Spirit-inspired from the heart of the heavenly Father to His children, to bring them into His magnificent presence and bless them richly.

As we begin expanding our horizons into the different forms of worship, such as prophetic dance, waving banners and shifting the atmosphere by blowing the shofar, we must also expand our vocabulary in our expression of worship. When we honor and praise God the Father in Hebrew, we can address Him as Yehovah, and when we address Him as our "El" we are expressing His Mightiness and Power. God is amazing, awesome and worthy to be praised in whatever language we choose to express our love for Him.

Song: Lord Most High

<u>El Elyon</u> is the Most High God who reigns with majesty, dominion and power.

You are my El Shaddai, you are My Elohim, Adonai

One day you set me free and gave me liberty.

And I praise your name

Lord Most High, Lord Most High

You gave your life for me

One day on Calvary and I hold you in high esteem.

You are the King of Kings

You are the Lord of Lords

And your awesomeness I can't explain. Lord Most High, Lord Most High

Bridge

There's no other like you

You are wonderful and true.

You are the alpha and omega

You're the beginning and the end.

(Repeat verse)

Most High, high, high

You are most high, high, high

You are my El

You are my El

You are my El

You are my El

You are my El, El, El

You are my El

You are higher than others

Matchless in power and might.

Oh yes, you're the Great I Am and for your kingdom I will stand.

Most High, Most High, Most High.

CHAPTER 1: THE CALL

Everyone called by God into the ministry of prophetic worship has a testimony to share on how they were called. My testimony begins with attending a praise and worship conference in Cranford, New Jersey. I was in the foyer during a break admiring the various shapes and colors of the banners (flags). As I picked up a red and gold fire-colored banner, I heard a soft voice behind me saying, "You are called to be a banner bearer."

She introduced herself and said her name was Patricia. She grabbed my hand gently and begin to pray boldly over me in tongues. As she prayed, the power and presence of the Holy Spirit begin to move all around us. After Patricia finished praying, she instructed me to take the banner and go into the conference room and begin to worship.

As I walked into the sanctuary, I asked myself, *What just happened?* I had no idea that an impartation had taken place.

Patricia picked up one of her large banners and begin to walk towards the front of the room. She then motioned for me to come up front with her. I had never worshipped with a banner before, but as I began to wave the banner I could feel the wind of the Holy Spirit blowing gently over me. At that very moment I felt the manifest presence of God and an immediate shift of the atmosphere in the room. In an instant, we shifted to a deeper level of praise and worship. Prophetic utterance began to come forth and I fell to my knees in reverence to an awesome, Holy God. At that very moment I knew within my spirit that I was truly called to be a worshipper.

Since that day many years ago, I have come to realize that worship is experienced and demonstrated from the depths of our being. It is not just about singing, dancing, or praying at a certain place or time. Worship is a mindset that is focused on our Creator for His goodness and His mercy. It is a heart that beats for God, to acknowledge Him and display our profound love for who is He is and for what He has done in our lives. True worship cannot be put in a box because it is a multi-dimensional, multifaceted expression of our sincere love for God. It is ever-changing and constantly evolving as God opens our eyes and hearts to reveal His nature and character.

My times of worship are very sacred to me. It is a place of intimacy where I can freely express my deepest feelings and emotions to the One who is the lover of my soul. It is a place of transparency; no masks are allowed -- only bare (Panin El Panin) face-to-face encounters with God. There are no holds barred; just total and complete surrender to my "Beloved."

"I am my beloved's, and his desire is for me." (Song of Solomon 7:10, NRSV) Surrender and humility are the focal points of all worship onto God. There is no place for pride or self-righteousness. Genuine heart-to-heart worship to the Lord should be the ruling passion and desire in the heart of every believer.

> Worship is the submission of all our nature to God. It is the quickening of conscience by His holiness, the nourishment of mind with his truth, the purifying of imagination by his beauty. The opening of the heart to His love, the surrender of will to His purpose- all of this gathered up in adoration, the most self-less emotion of which our nature is capable.[1]

William Temple, Archbishop of Canterbury

You come to a place of knowing that worship is not some exercise or regimented routine that we go through. It is a deep yearning in your spirit to demonstrate your love, gratitude, and thanksgiving to our Heavenly Father for His extravagant attention and love that He showers on us continually. We can live a life of abundance, blessings and fulfill our divine destiny and purpose here in the earth. For us to accomplish this, praise and worship must become a lifestyle and not something we do only on Sunday mornings. Once you recognize and accept your true life's purpose, it is easy to walk into your God-designed destiny.

A Download from Heaven

Allow God to crack open the core of your innermost being, so He can pour the balm of love and affection into you as you praise and worship Him. As love recognizing love begins to flow, your soul realizes and releases a deep appreciation and gratitude for who He is and for what He has done in your life. You then release your love unto Him unconditionally with no constraints or holding anything back. You are honoring Him for being the Great Majesty, the King of all creation, the One who sits upon the throne of Royalty and Grace. This is the baring of one's soul!

Song: Speak to My Heart Lord

"Give me ears to hear clearly and an obedient heart to follow your guidance and direction."

Your servant is listening to what you have to say.

Consecrate my heart oh Lord and sanctify my ways.

I'll go where you send me and speak your word of Truth.

Just pour out your anointing I just want to be used by you.

I've been through the fire; the dross is burned away.

For in the Holy of Holies only purity can stay.

The power of your Word Lord is like a two-edged sword.

Cutting and dividing, it never comes back void.

I stand on your Word now; you've never failed me yet.

Your wisdom and counsel my heart cannot reject.

Awaken the spirit the slumbers deep inside

A face-to-face encounter, no longer will I hide. I won't hide from you.

I bow in reverence before the righteous King.

Through the blood of Jesus my soul has been redeemed.

Forgiveness and Mercy has covered all my sins.

With the power of your Spirit my new life can begin. New life, new life, new life.

Bridge

Speak to my heart Lord and draw me near, whisper softly the words I long to hear, You love me, You'll never leave me alone, never alone, alone.

Let your words pierce their hearts and turn them around from their wayward ways.

Lord speak, Lord speak, let me be your mouthpiece. Speeeak

Speak to my heart Lord, Speak to my heart Lord, Speak to my heart Lord-ord.

Reflections

Chapter 2: Shifting the Atmosphere Through Worship

An atmosphere is described as the present tone or mood of a place or situation. Every time we praise, we worship, or pray, we invite the atmosphere of heaven into the earth. Praise, worship, and prayer have the power to penetrate and shift the physical presence and mood of any room or space. We can shift the atmosphere in our home, church, workplace or school through praise and worship. Too many of us just settle for the way things are in the natural world, not realizing that heaven is waiting for an invitation to come in and restructure the ambivalence in our lives.

Many believers are not aware that they can create an atmosphere that ushers in the manifested presence of God. Praise and worship elevate us into the presence and power of God. Worship also releases the power of the Holy Spirit to break all bondages, stagnation and hindrances. When we become aware that our praise manifests God's presence, we begin to realize that praise repels the presence of the enemy, known as Satan. An atmosphere that is filled and charged with sincere worship and praise to God with a humble and contrite heart is disgusting to demonic powers. Satan fears the power in the name of Jesus and flees from the habitation of the Lord's praise. Demonic activity is arrested, and warring angelic hosts are released to fight on your behalf. All forms of captive resistance must release their hold over your life.

We find an example of powerful, atmospheric-shifting praise in Acts 16:25-26. This account in Acts relates an unusual and powerful incident that happened in the prison where Paul and Silas were being held.

> And at midnight Paul and Silas prayed, and sang praises unto God: and the prisoners heard them. And suddenly there was a great earthquake, so that the foundations of the prison were shaken: and immediately all the doors were opened, and everyone's bands were loosed.
>
> (Acts 16:25-26, KJV)

Paul and Silas used the power of prayer and song as they praised and worshipped God. Through their praise and worship, they surrendered and elevated their hearts above their situation and entered the presence of God. In turn, their Heavenly Father provided a conduit for His power to manifest and operate in their circumstances. Paul and Silas knew the secret of how to operate by using worship to enter into the presence of God (beyond their trials and tribulations), where all things are possible. The Bible tells us in Psalm 22:3 (KJV) that when we praise God, He inhabits the praises of His people.

Establishing the Reign of the Kingdom

Jesus came to establish the reign of His Kingdom when He came into the earthly realm and paid the price for our sins. He made it possible for us to approach the throne of grace and mercy. We can come boldly into the presence of our Heavenly Father in a posture of lavish praise and worship to Him. As we worship God, He reciprocates by releasing a huge tidal wave of His strength and glory. This is a place that God inhabits, and His abiding presence resides. This is a place of adoration, rest, and trust in Him. We enter a place of love and empowerment, which ushers us into a deeper level of intimacy with Him.

What does it mean that God "inhabits the praises of His people?" How does this impact our relationship with the Creator? The word inhabits or enthrone in Hebrew is "yashab," which means that God rests in, sits upon, dwells within the adoration and worship of His people.[2] He is present and glorified when we sing praises about Him and bless His holy name. As we draw nigh to Him, He draws nearer to us during our praise.

Psalm chapter 22:3-5 reminds us that God is always listening and is very much present. Even if He feels far away, He is not. He desires our praise and worship in all things; in the sunshine and in the storm. He is always there when we need Him.

Praise is the catalyst that invites the presence of God to abide in our midst. It has been noted that praise has the power to shift the molecular structure in any space and time, so "The King of Glory" can come in to manifest His rule and authority - to touch, heal and bring deliverance to His people. God's glory is all-encompassing and invasive; anything in the immediate environment that is not yielding to His power and authority cannot stand. If you take the time to create a spiritual atmosphere which attracts God's presence, He will draw near to you. Your communication with Him will be rich and meaningful. "Draw near to God and He will draw near to you." (James 4:8, NASB1995)

Nothing can compare to being in the presence of our compassionate, loving Heavenly Father. When we worship God in spirit and in truth, He is pleased. Just as an earthly father delights in the love of his children, God gets immense joy when we shower Him with our love and praise. In turn, He responds with showers of love and blessings.

The past two years have presented many challenges as we adjusted to "our new normal" post-pandemic way of life. Many of us are feeling tired, weary, and fatigued by the battle of our daily lives. Sometimes it is difficult to maintain a positive mindset as you put one foot in front of the other just to make it through the day. There seems to be no light at the end of the tunnel, only pervading darkness with no relief or breakthrough in sight. The good news is that you do not have to live under a dark cloud of oppression, depression, and anxiety. During these times of uncertainty, chaos, and the constant shifting in the environment, we must make it our priority and goal to cling fiercely and stubbornly to God in the good times as well as in challenging times.

Pushing Back the Powers of Darkness

Your praise is a powerful weapon that can push back the powers of darkness and block the hissing lies and attacks of the adversary. Demonic forces cannot stand around when we are praising God, because He is actively fighting our battles. We see an example of God's fierce power to fight our battles in 2 Chronicles 20 as King Jehoshaphat was trembling with fear as he faced a vast army coming against him. He lifted a prayer and praise to the God of his fathers in obedience to the prophetic word of the Lord given to him by Jahaziel (a descendant from the sons of Asaph).

What an unusual way to start a battle. The tribe of Judah were facing three armies that were determined to wipe them off the face of the earth. Instead of putting powerful warriors on the frontline, King Jehoshaphat chose anointed minstrels and singers. The singers and minstrels were not praying and petitioning God to protect them and give them a victory. Instead, they lifted their voices in a loud praise to Him for His faithful love and compassion toward them. The God of Israel had promised to deliver them from the hands of their enemies. They sang with their hearts and souls: "Give thanks to the Lord, for His lovingkindness is everlasting." (2 Chronicles 20:21b, NASB)

They all stood in awe as they witnessed God defeat their enemies miraculously because they were obedient to praise Him during a seemingly impossible situation.

What battles are you now facing? Perhaps you are battling an addiction, a life-threatening illness, or a sinful habit that seems impossible to overcome despite your best efforts. Whatever the circumstance may be, no matter what you are facing, remember, "The Battle is the Lord's!" (1 Samuel 17:47, KJV)

Believe in Him as the tribe of Judah did. Do not wait to see what the results will be; praise Him now and stand in awe as you watch Him fight on your behalf.

Song: Shifting the Atmosphere - Hear Ye O Israel

"Hear, O Israel: The Lord our God is one Lord"

(Deuteronomy 6:4, KJV)

God is calling His people back to Him, to return to their first love.

Hear Ye O Israel, Hear Ye O Israel, Yahweh is our Elohim, Yahweh is One -He is One

Hear Ye O Israel, Yahweh is our Elohim, Yahweh is One- Wake up, wake up, wake up Hear Ye O Israel, Yahweh is our Elohim, Yahweh is One- He is One

And you shall love Yahweh your Elohim with all your mind, all your heart and your soul

Hallelujah, hallelujah, hallelujah, hallelujah.

Then repeat the first stanzas -

Hear Ye O Israel, Yahweh is our Elohim, Yahweh is One (4 times).

Then repeat chorus:

And you shall love Yahweh your Elohim. (4 times)

Hallelujah, hallelujah, hallelujah, Hallelujah.

End with:

Yahweh is our Elohim, Yahweh is One.

Reflections

CHAPTER 3: WORSHIP IN HOLY REVERENCE – SILENCE AND MEDITATION

"But the Lord is in His holy abode. Be silent before Him all the earth."

Habakkuk 2:20 – The Jewish Bible Tanakh The Holy Scriptures (pg. 1067)

Think back for a moment: when was the last time you really experienced silence and solitude? We live in a world where we are bombarded constantly with noise and distractions all around us, whether it be from our mobile devices, television, or social media. The pace of our hectic schedules and busyness eliminates the much-needed time in quietness and silence. Psalm 46:10 (KJV) commands us to "Be still and know that I am God."

Being silent seems to have a negative connotation, and much of the time, silence is avoided intentionally. However, embracing silence and solitude creates a longing to dig deeper into the depths of our souls. It is a private place and time alone with God. In this place, God can speak and we can quiet our spirits to listen to His voice. God is allowed to be the Communicator as we listen intently to Him. There is a place within you that is private and reserved for times that only you and God can share. As we sit in silence, the tangible presence of God is felt as we quiet our thoughts and focus our prayers and attention on Him. Silence is a powerful expression of our worship to God, and it is often the missing link if we desire to be on a deeper level of intimacy with Him.

"My soul, wait in silence for God only, For my hope is from Him. He only is my rock and salvation, My stronghold; I shall not be shaken." (Psalm 62: 5-6, NASB1995)

King David is a prime example of someone who knew how to quiet his spirit so that he could experience the power and presence of God. David exemplifies to us how we are to wait in silence before God. He meditated on the word of God to still his spirit as he received revelation and insight into the nature and heart of God.

Silence is a key element in worship. Silence teaches us that prayer is not just a conversation involving words, but it is also a posture of being open and receptive to hear the voice of God. In this posture of silence, we acknowledge that He is God, and we are not. We surrender our will and our hearts to be awed by the "King of Kings," the Lover of our soul. Sometimes spoken words cannot express our love and adoration to the awesomeness of God.

> Hunger for God requires the cultivation of silence. Even in engagement, crisis, and activity, we need to seek the inner space where we can be sustained and renewed. This is a time we allow God to do what he needs to do in transforming and changing our lives in accordance with His divine will and plan.[3]
>
> Diana L. Eck

During my times of silent mediative worship, I quiet my thoughts and shut out all the cares and worries of the world around me. In this place of solitude, I focus my prayers and thoughts on God. I am often overwhelmed and brought to tears as His loving presence permeates the room. It is during these intimate times that I know my Heavenly Father loves me unconditionally and my response to Him is passionate worship. In the absence of spoken words, silence is the purest form of worship to a Holy God. It is in this place where peace and tranquility surpasses all understanding.

I encourage you to begin spending a solid amount of time in solitude. Begin setting aside some time to sit quietly in the presence of God a few minutes each day. Use this time to shut down your "to-do list" and just focus on allowing God to speak to your heart. He will show you the areas in your life that you need to focus on and the things you need to let go. We must remember even Yeshua (Jesus) our Messiah withdrew from the crowds and took time to go to a place of solitude to be with His Heavenly Father.

We all need to give our undivided attention to God by being still in our heart and mind. Times of silent worship and meditation opens our mind and heart so that we can hear clearly and make sound decisions, which gives us divine direction and orders our footsteps to where God has chosen for us. Silent worship and meditation press us to reach down into the deeper recesses of our soul and spirit to appreciate and acknowledge God's love and grace toward us. We have time to reflect on the situations, circumstances, and trials from which He has delivered us, and how His strong arm of protection has kept us safe. It brings us to our knees in gratitude and appreciation as we realize the depth of God's love and that He is ever-present to help us whenever we need Him.

When we worship in silence, in this sacred space that you have intentionally set aside time to meet with the Lord, you surrender, unplug, and withdraw from all the busyness of life. This is a non-judgmental zone and a place where you can let your hair down and bare your soul to the One who will love you just as you are.

Song: He Who Dwells - Psalm 91

We are safe and secure under the shield and protection of our Heavenly Father.

"The name of the Lord is a strong tower, the righteous run into it and they are safe." (Proverbs18:10, KJV, paraphrased by author)

He who dwells in the secret place

Shall abide under His Shadow (4 times)

O Yahweh, O Yahweh, O Yahweh, O Yahweh, O Yahweh, O Yahweh, O Yahweh, O

He who dwells in the secret place

Shall abide under His shadow (4times)

In the darkness of the night, you surround me.

Under the shield of your wings, I will abide.

In the secret place is where you hide me.

A place that gives me the strength to overcome.

He who dwells, He who dwells Shall be comforted
He who dwells, He who dwells Shall be safe

He who dwells, He who dwells

Shall be healed

For he rests in the wings of your grace, for he rests in
the wings of your grace.

He who dwells in the secret place.

Shall abide under His shadow (4 times)

O Yahweh, O Yahweh, O Yahweh, O Yahweh, O
Yahweh, O Yahweh, O Yahweh, O

Reflections

Chapter 4: Worship Through Movement – Prophetic Dance

"Let them praise His name with dancing."
(Psalm 149:3, NASB)

It was through an impartation from a profound prophetic dancer/banner bearer that awakened my gift of prophetic dance. I had taken ballet and jazz dance lessons as a little girl, but those genres of dance could not compare or prepare me for the exhilarating joy I felt as I ministered in prophetic dance before the Lord. There was no rehearsed movement; just free-flowing praise and worship orchestrated through the unction of the Holy Spirit. I felt no limitations or restrictions as I leaped, twirled, extended my hands, and ministered before the Lord. There was a synchronization of the anointing of the Holy Spirit and the prophetic dance that ushered me into a dimension of high praise, adoration, and love for my Heavenly Father, which is hard to express in words.

In this place of exalted worship there is only the Heavenly audience of you and the Lord. The earthly audience seems to fade into the background, and it is just you, glorifying the Most High God. The ministry of prophetic dance is an expression of worship, which involves the incorporation of your whole physical being (all that is within you). It is a beautiful expression of our love, reverence and adoration to God through flowing dance movements.

What does it mean to bless the Lord with all that is within you? Once again, I will use King David who was a true worshipper. He worshipped God with boundless freedom.

"And David was dancing before the LORD with all his might, and David was wearing a linen ephod. So David and all the house of Israel brought up the ark of the LORD with shouting and the sound of the trumpet." (2 Samuel 6:14-15, NASB)

King David was a worshipper, who worshiped God with extreme measures.

> Dance enables us to enter a level of worship that encompasses all that is within us as we worship, not only in spirit and soul, but also as we respond in adoration through the expression of our physical bodies.[4]
>
> Dr. Ann Stevenson

When I minister in the presence of Almighty God through prophetic dance, I feel as if I am being transported into a powerful whirlwind as the Holy Spirit begins to flow and move through my prophetic dance expressions of worship. The more yielded I am to the Holy Spirit, the greater His power and presence as He ministers to the hearts and souls of the people. As a prophetic dancer, you must be a yielded vessel in the hands of God and flow with the wind of the Spirit as you worship. The prophetic dance conveys powerful messages that cannot always be expressed through spoken words. This communication is Spirit to spirit, where the Holy Spirit is conveying the prophetic word of the Lord to his people.

As you are tuned in to the movement of the Holy Spirit, the realm of heaven is released in the earth. This is a powerful place of ministry because this is where we witness the manifested presence of the Lord as He releases a prophetic word or a vision.

There is also an anointing through the prophetic dance that releases the power of God to heal, comfort, and bring deliverance through undoing, destroying, and binding the works of the enemy. This is a depth of prophetic dance that is executed with authority, power, and purpose. As we minister in alignment with certain anointed songs and music, that power is released in our dance through the unction of the Holy Spirit and the will of God.

There are several types of dance movements you may see ministered by the prophetic dancer.

1. There is the dance of praise, where you may leap and jump, with steps and movements given to you as the Holy Spirit leads as you offer up praise and thanksgiving to the Lord. "Praise Him with the timbrel and dancing." (Psalm 150:4, NASB)

2. There is the warfare dance that is exem-

plified by stomping, clapping, marching, pushing, and pulling. This warfare dance is ministered to break demonic oppression and spiritual bondage of the enemy that is discerned in the atmosphere. There is also an anointing in the warfare dance that releases deliverance, healing, and breakthrough. I minister the warfare dance when I discern oppressive spirits in the atmosphere that must be commanded to leave.

3. Then there is the dance of worship as we humble ourselves in the presence of God. It is during this time that you bow in reverence and adoration to the "King of Kings." The movements of my worship dance are soft, slow, and flowing as I lavish my love and adoration on my Heavenly Father. As I worship God, there is a spirit-to-Spirit connection, and it is here in

His presence that I can hear Him speak to me clearly.

The next time you are listening to anointed worship music and you feel the flow of the Holy Spirit, begin to move your hands and your feet. Do not be afraid to get up and move your body in a prophetic dance before the Lord. You may find yourself caught up in the wind of the Spirit and you will be amazed at the freedom in this form of worship. It is a beautiful expression of your love and adoration to God for His goodness and blessings in your life.

Flowing with Banners

"We will sing for joy over your victory and the name of our God we will set up our banners." (Psalm 20:5a, NASB)

The ministry of the "Banner or Standard Bearer" is highly effective in the front line of worship, praise, warfare, intercession, and prophecy. You may ask what is a standard? The Bible uses the word standard or banner to describe what we call a flag. Many people identify and refer to the ministry of the banner or standard bearer as the "flag ministry." I am a standard bearer and I love to minister with banners of all shapes, colors, and sizes. This is a powerful ministry which is sensitive to the guidance of the Holy Spirit. The individual or vessel who uses the banners should be in prayer, consecrated and totally surrendered to the will of God. It is important that they study the Word of God because God speaks to us through His Word. It is impossible to interpret the move of God without being familiar with His Word.

Banner bearers are instruments of praise and worship as they welcome the presence of the Spirit of God. They are alert and know how to flow as the Holy Spirit directs them. In unison with the Holy Spirit, colors, music, and movement can be interpreted prophetically, and declared. The banner bearer must stay focused and attentive to the leading of the Holy Spirit to be effective in their ministry. In this posture of worship, the banner bearer also stands as an intercessor for themselves and the people in their presence. As they wave their colorful, flowing banners and minister in prophetic dance, their worship charges the atmosphere for the power of the Holy Spirit to minister to the needs of the people to break bondages, usher in deliverance, and release stagnation and hindrances. Demonic activity must cease, and the warring angels are released to fight on behalf of the people of God.

Ministering with the banners is incredibly special to me. As I wave the banners, I am also listening to the guidance and direction of the Holy Spirit. Revelation knowledge is imparted as to what patterns to wave my banners and what prayers of intercession are needed for God to bless His people.

Spiritual direction is also given as to what color banners should be waved in combination with specific prophetic movements. In this dimension of worship, the banner has a voice to speak from the heart of God and true prophetic interpretation goes forth. Who could imagine that a flowing piece of cloth in the hands of an anointed servant could have such a powerful impact on the people gathered in the presence of God?

There are numerous ways that the voice of the banner speaks and declares the presence and power of God.

The breath of the Holy Spirit blows on the fabric and the banner bearer is obedient to His flow, direction, and movement. They are given insight as to what color, shape, and size banner to wave. The assorted colors, shapes and sizes of the banners symbolize the ministry needs of the people.

1. A waving red banner represents the power

of the blood of Jesus for deliverance and salvation (2 Chronicles 7:14-15). It is a reminder to the Body of Christ that we need to seek God's face and repent from everything that is not in alignment with His will and His Word. It is also waved for engagement in spiritual warfare and dispatching angelic warriors.

2. A waving white banner acknowledges the presence and power of a Holy God in our midst. God gave Moses and the armies of Israel a great victory as Moses raised his rod. After the battle, Moses built an altar and called it "Yehovah Nissi" – "The-Lord-is-my-Banner" (Exodus 17:15).

3. A waving yellow and orange banner alerts us to God's healing power in our presence to release healing and miracles (Psalm

103:3).

4. A waving pink banner is used when we are in a posture of prayer and intercession as we offer our prayer and prophetic intercession to God and wave our banners before Him to communicate the cry of our hearts. When the banner bearer is standing as an intercessor, they receive revelation from the Holy Spirit concerning the spiritual atmosphere, which leads them to pray, intercede and engage in spiritual warfare. God's love and compassion is also demonstrated with waving a pink banner as the banner bearer prays for God's lovingkindness, forgiveness, grace, and mercy to touch the hearts of the people (Psalm 51:16-17).

5. When I wave the blue banner, the wind of the Holy Spirit and the atmosphere of

Heaven invade that space and ministering angels are present.

6. When I raise the purple or gold banners, they point to the "Great Majesty," the Creator of the heavens and the earth. I am declaring God's sovereignty in that atmosphere (Psalm 24:8).

The ministry of the banner bearer always points to God our Heavenly Father. We worship Him in spirit and in truth and identify ourselves as children of the Most High God through Jesus Christ our Lord and Savior. It is not just pageantry; it is a ministry that honors God as He speaks to us through color, movement, and sound. Lifting a standard/banner is not limited to a congregational setting. You can worship in your home, the geographical territory assigned to you, or in a public gathering as the Spirit of God leads you.

Song: We've Come to Worship

The true sons and daughters of God will enter His presence and worship Him in spirit and in truth.

We've come to worship, worship you

We've come to worship, worship you

You are Yeshua, Ha'Mashiach

We bow before your throne.

We've come to sing a song of praise

We've come to sing a song of praise

You are Yeshua, Ha'Mashiach

The Ancient One of Days.

Worship, Worship, in that secret place

Worship, Worship, we long to seek your face.

We've come to lavish you with love.

We've come to lavish you with love.

You are Yeshua, Ha'Mashiach

Holy One from up above.

Worship, Worship we stand in awe of you.

Worship, Worship the righteous One of Truth

Worship, Worship in that secret place

Worship, Worship

We long to seek your face

We long to seek your face

We long to seek your face.

Reflections

Chapter 5: Worship in Songs of Praise - The Song of the Lord

"Sing to the Lord a new song; sing to the LORD, all the earth." (Psalm 96:1, NIV)

What would the world be like without music? Music is a powerful way to reach the very depth of your soul and emotions. It can bring peace and comfort to your heart. Music consoles in times of grief, loneliness, and despair. It can take you soaring to unimaginable heights of happiness and joy. Music is a stress reliever, which allows you to release your frustration and anger in a safe way. The beat of the music can also encourage you to get your body moving and help improve your health and well-being. Music is known to have a healing and therapeutic aspect, where it lowers the blood pressure to recalibrate your mental and physical health.

There is a deep thread that runs between the fabric of music and worship.

God created the wonderful sounds of music and songs so that we can worship Him, because we were created to worship Him. Our Heavenly Father loves beautiful music and songs. He sits on his throne of glory surrounded by heavenly melodic voices and songs. Music and song are an awesome form of worship. I have been singing since the age of three and I have sung in various concerts, music events, in the church choir and on the worship team. Nothing gives me more gratification than when I worship the Lord in song. It is a gift that He was given to me to pour out my love and adoration onto Him and to bring those listening into His manifested presence.

I read a book a while ago written by Apostle John Eckhardt entitled "The Spirit of Asaph." This powerful book brought so much revelation regarding the psalmist anointing on my life. I finally found the words to describe my music ministry. God spoke to me and revealed to me that I was an Asaph prophet. I learned that the family of Asaph carried the mantle of worship, and they stood before the Ark of the Covenant continually singing songs to the Lord. "But Asaph made music with cymbals; Benaiah and Jahaziel the priests regularly blew the trumpets before the ark of the covenant of God." (1 Chronicles 16:5-6, NKJV)

Apostle Eckhardt also noted that the spirit of Asaph has a grace to gather the people into the presence of God, where miracles and the glory of God are manifested. It is no coincidence that the enemy fights so fiercely against the flow of prophetic music because he knows the power of the anointing and revelation that is released through it.

You may now be asking, why is the song of the Lord or prophetic singing so important to the believer? Prophetic singing (The Song of the Lord) is a prophetic utterance which is composed and flows by the inspiration of the Holy Spirit. It is a prophetically-inspired song which has never been sung before. As the psalmist and minstrels minister the song of the Lord, an open heaven and the glory of God charge the atmosphere with His power and presence.

Singing the song of the Lord requires you to be sensitive in the Spirit to:

1. Release a word of prophecy- a song which can give instruction and direction.

2. Release a word of encouragement- a

song where we receive God's encouraging words.

3. Release a word of comfort- a song that brings God's comfort during times of trials, challenges, and sorrow.

4. Release a word of exhortation- a song that focuses on our walk with the Lord and prompts us to fulfill His plan and purpose in our lives. During this time of prophetic worship through the song of the Lord, we are singing Heavenly melodies, words and songs that not only minister to those in our presence, but also unto our Heavenly Father.

Singing the Song of the Lord is not limited to psalmists and minstrels in the church. God can breathe a song through anyone who is open and receptive to release a prophetic utterance in song composed by the inspiration of the Holy Spirit. This worship is free and liberating, which breaks you out of religious constraints so that you can truly worship God in Spirit and in Truth.

Songs of Thanksgiving

"Enter into His gates with thanksgiving, and into His courts with praise: Be thankful unto him, and bless his name." (Psalm 100:4, KJV)

Songs of thanksgiving ascribe to God's deeds and focus on what He has done for us. We thank him not only for ourselves but for His matchless works and deeds in the lives of our families, friends, communities, and churches. The Word commands that we come into His presence with singing and thanksgiving. We sing songs of thanksgiving because we love God for who He is and for His unfailing faithfulness and love that He continues to show us. When I sing songs of thanksgiving to God, whether in private or in an assembly, I am expressing my gratitude to Him for His grace and His goodness in my life. I am thankful for what He has already done, and it does not take much for me to get excited about what He is doing in my present moment. All my attention is directed towards showing God reverence as I open my mouth to sing and give Him the highest praise. A posture of thanksgiving in song releases/activates your faith and directs your focus on the power and presence of God in your life and not on the problems and hardships that you may be facing. As we sing songs of thanksgiving, we open the doors to the miracle-working power of God to be manifested in our presence.

When we sing songs of thanksgiving, we also put the adversary on notice, because our songs can be weapons of warfare to quench the fiery darts and dismantle evil agendas and plans. Satan knows the supernatural power of music, which can break through demonic barriers and strongholds. His feeble attempts to hold us in a state of fear and anxiety are released as we elevate our thanksgiving and praise up to God. Thanksgiving reminds us that we are victorious when we exalt God and turn our attention to His ability to turn impossible situations and circumstances around on our behalf. Our song of thanksgiving is a catalyst that prepares us to witness the miracle-working power of God in our lives.

"Oh, give thanks to the LORD, for *He is* good! For His mercy endures forever." (1 Chronicles 16:34, NKJV)

During these times of chaos, uncertainty, and in constantly shifting and changing environments, you must make it your goal to cling to God fiercely and stubbornly. You cannot let trials, suffering, and challenging times drive a wedge between you and God. This is a wonderful opportunity to seek

Him and draw close to Him with all your heart through your praise and worship. Praise and worship Him for His goodness and grace that sustains and shields you under the shadow of His wings of protection and safety. Despite what you see happening in the world with your natural eyes, focus your spiritual eyes and hold fast to your faith because God is still sovereign and rules with power and dominion. Keep your praise and worship always in your mouth and release it into His ears. God hears you, and He will respond with His manifest presence and power in your midst. As you praise and worship Him, He will give you renewed strength, a second wind to press on and the determination not to quit despite the tough times you are facing. Let your life be a song of praise and worship to God.

Authentic worship cannot be pigeon-holed into a single expression. It is expressed in a variety of ways. When you walk into the throne room of

God, it is filled with opulence and beauty. The colors and beauty are amazing and breathtaking to behold. There is a sense of awe and reverence when you are in The Presence of the King, who sits on the Throne of Glory.

This is the Beauty of Worship.

Reflections

About the Author

Dwendolyn Andrea Tatum is an inspiring psalmist, songwriter, and prophetic worshipper. Her worship through song and prophetic dance is heartfelt and invites you to experience the glory and presence of God.

As a young child growing up in North Carolina, "Andrea," as she is fondly known, was always aware of the call of God upon her life. She is a graduate of the University of North Carolina in Greensboro, where she received a Bachelor of Science Degree in Nursing. Andrea is also an ordained minister with a Master of Divinity Degree from Drew University School of Theology in Madison, New Jersey.

Andrea has ministered in song and prophetic dance at numerous churches, gospel concerts and musical events in the New York, New Jersey and Maryland areas, and in Israel.

This is her first book release; however, she released her first CD entitled "Enter In" in 2012, which is a selection of Holy Spirit-inspired songs.

Andrea's heart desire is to see the manifested presence of God touching, healing and delivering His people in an atmosphere of praise and worship. Andrea retired recently from a nursing career in the New Jersey Public School System. She has a son, a daughter, two grandchildren and an adorable dog named "Rocket," who is a great inspiration.

Andrea gives all the glory and praise to God.

AFTERWORD

While working on this project, "The Beauty of Worship, In the Presence of the King," I was thoroughly moved by Dwendolyn Andrea's story of how the Lord sent someone into her life who recognized that she had a calling.

Many of us go through life without understanding the purpose that the Lord has set out for us to pursue. Now, there are many directions one can follow. Are we to wed and have children? Are we to remain single? Are we to follow a particular profession that we are passionate about learning and centering our career around? Or are we called by the Lord to minister to his people in a church setting?

Imagine trusting the word of a stranger, "You are called to be a Banner Bearer." How would you have responded? Through her faith, Andrea picked up the banner and walked to the front of the church, and without training she followed the unction of Holy Spirit.

Dwendolyn Andrea Tatum has definitely found her place in this realm. She is a dynamic praise and worship minister. She explains how the Holy Spirit guides and directs her every move, and describes her prayers of intercession as she ministers.

Have you ever had a strong urge to do something that you had never done before in front of your congregation or at a gathering of people who you may or may not know?

I have stood on the pulpit of my church, Green Grove Baptist, in West Berlin, New Jersey, and presented two or three messages. I am called to be a scribe. I will research Scripture and put a lesson together. Yet, when asked by my pastor to consider joining the ministry as a minister, I did not feel that it was right for me.

I did, however, teach in our Spiritual Fitness class for a month on Spiritual Gifts. I felt the Holy Spirit with me each step of the way preparing for the month-long class, and I had time to rehearse. However, Andrea did not rehearse or even have time to think and reflect on whether becoming a Banner Bearer was right for her, or if it was just something she wanted to try.

There was no try; she just did it. "The Beauty of Worship" is a beautiful illustration of how one individual heard the call from God, and because of her obedience, she has blessed many people.

You can hear her perform the songs listed at the end of each chapter. Her YouTube channel can be found by going to YouTube and searching for

Andrea Tatum – Lord Most High or by following this link:

https://bit.ly/musicbyandreatatum

Here are nine verses to help you be in the presence of the Lord.

May you learn to be still and listen to His voice.

"The Sovereign Lord has given me his words of wisdom, so that I know how to comfort the weary. Morning by morning he wakens me and opens my understanding to his will." (Isaiah 50:4, NLT)

"'Call to me and I will answer you and tell you great and unsearchable things you do not know.'" (Jeremiah 33:3, NIV)

"He says, 'Be still, and know that I am God; I will be exalted among the nations,
I will be exalted in the earth.'" (Psalm 46:10, NIV)

"As the deer pants for streams of water, so my soul pants for you, my God. My soul thirsts for God, for the living God. When can I go and meet with God?" (Psalm 42:1-2, NIV)

"How lovely is your dwelling place, Lord Almighty! My soul yearns, even faints, for the courts of the Lord..." (Psalm 84:1-2, NIV)

"Come near to God and he will come near to you. Wash your hands, you sinners, and purify your hearts, you double-minded." (James 4:8, NIV)

"'I am the vine; you are the branches. If you remain in me and I in you, you will bear much fruit; apart from me you can do nothing.'" (John 15:5, NIV)

"My heart says of you, 'Seek his face!' Your face, Lord, I will seek." (Psalm 27:8, NIV)

"Therefore, brothers and sisters, since we have confidence to enter the Most Holy Place by the blood of Jesus... let us draw near to God with a sincere heart and with the full assurance that faith brings, having our hearts sprinkled to cleanse us from a guilty conscience and having our bodies washed with pure water." (Hebrews 10:19 & 22, NIV)

Respectfully,

Deborah Smart, Author and Publisher

REFERENCES

1. Sohn, P. (2014, January 13). *William Temple on Worship*. Paul Sohn. https://paulsohn.org/william-temple-on-worship/

2. *Strong's Hebrew: 3427. (yashab) -- to sit, remain, dwell*. (n.d.). https://biblehub.com/hebrew/3427.htm

3. Diana L. Eck, Encountering God, a Spiritual Journey from Bozeman to Banaras (Boston, Mass.: Beacon Press, 1993), 154.

4. Dr. Ann Stevenson, Dance! God's Holy Purpose (Shippensburg, PA: Destiny Image,1998), 82

www.ingramcontent.com/pod-product-compliance
Lightning Source LLC
Chambersburg PA
CBHW060338130626
46553CB00003B/1043